WHEN THOMAS EDISON FED SOMEONE WORMS

by Mark Weakland

Illustrated by Thomas Radcliffe

PICTURE WINDOW BOOKS

a capstone imprint

Thomas Alva Edison was the seventh child of Samuel and Nancy Edison. He was born on a winter day in 1847. Everyone called Thomas "Little Al."

"How's my little Al?" his dad would ask. In time his father would answer that question with "curious" and "smart." These words would describe Thomas Edison for the rest of his life.

As a man Edison became a great inventor and businessman. His success grew from the curiosity, smarts, and wonder he showed as a child.

When Thomas Edison was very young, his parents took him to his sister's farm. Little Thomas wandered off to play. When he failed to come back, his sister and her husband grew worried.

They found Thomas in the barn, sitting happily on the goose's nest!

"I saw baby chickens come out of eggs the old hen was sitting on," Thomas said, "so I thought I could make little gooses come out of the goose eggs if I sat on them. If the hens and geese can do it, why can't I?"

Little Al lived with his family in Milan, Ohio. The town was a grain center and port. Wheat was brought in by wagons, stored in bins, and shipped out by boats.

There were grain bins near Little Al's home. As a boy he played among them. He would walk the rims, waving his arms to keep his balance.

One day Little Al lost his balance and fell in a bin! Luckily, someone rescued him before he was harmed.

Little Al loved to wander down to the Milan shipyards. He liked to watch the men building boats. He often peppered them with questions.

"He's as inquisitive as a young red squirrel!" exclaimed one man.

"He's a nervous little question-box," said another.

Maybe Little Al asked the men about the shape of the boats. Perhaps he asked about the tools they used to build them. Or maybe he wanted to know how boats float.

9

There were other places to explore besides the grain bins and shipyards. Once while exploring a pasture, Little Al discovered a bee's nest. He crouched down to observe it and focused hard on the bees. He didn't even see the ram that lived in the pasture.

Al got a nasty surprise when the ram chased him!

"Baa!" bleated the ram.

"*Mama!*" yelled Al.

11

At age 7, Little Al and his family moved to Port Huron, Michigan. He continued to be curious, especially about birds. Little Al observed two things about birds. First, birds flew. Second, birds ate worms.

"I bet birds fly because they eat worms," Little Al thought. "Maybe worms will make people fly too."

To test his theory, he mashed up worms.

Then he blended the goop with water. Finally he asked a girl to drink his special mixture. The girl who drank the worms did not fly, but she did get sick!

Little Al also tested his theory of flight on an old friend. He knew that Seidlitz powder made gas. Little Al asked his buddy to swallow the powder. He thought that maybe it would make his friend fly. This trick did not work either, and the boy never flew.

Little Al wasn't just curious about flight. He was also interested in communication. As an experiment, he and his friend, John Clancy, built a telegraph line. It ran for 1 mile (1.6 kilometer) through woods between their homes.

To test the line, the two boys
sent newspaper stories to each
other. The line worked!

For most of his life, Little Al was homeschooled by his mother.

At home he spent happy hours reading.

He also enjoyed creating things and solving problems.

He made electrical toys and experimented with magnets. He also collected materials for his chemistry projects.

When his supplies cluttered the house, his mother said,
"Take it to the basement, Al!"
In the basement Little Al had a quiet place to work.

Thomas was a boy who had a knack for business. He started by getting a job as a "candy butcher" when he was 12 years old. A "candy butcher" was a person who sold things to train passengers. From 7:00 a.m. until 9:00 p.m. daily, Thomas worked a train that traveled between Port Huron and Detroit, Michigan.

"Magazines! Newspapers!" he called, strolling up and down the aisle. He peddled candy, cigars, and peanuts. And he had fruit, sandwiches, joke books, and many other things to sell too.

Thomas set up a printing press in a train car. When the train stopped between cities, Thomas wrote articles. He printed them in a newspaper he called *The Weekly Herald*. Then he sold the newspaper on the train.

He also set up a small chemistry lab in a train car. When a chemistry experiment once started a fire on the train, Thomas was in big trouble. "Get off this train!" yelled the conductor.

All of Thomas' things were dumped onto the nearest train platform. That was the end of the chemistry experiments on the train. But Thomas continued to work as a "candy butcher."

Working for the railroad brought Thomas good luck too. One day a 3-year-old boy wandered in front of a runaway boxcar. Sprinting, Thomas grabbed the little boy and carried him to safety.

The boy's father happened to be the telegraph operator at the railroad station. "I'd like to repay you," said the grateful man. "I'll teach you how to run a telegraph."

"It's a deal!" said Thomas.

TELEGRAMS

Thomas was a telegraph operator by the age of 15. For the next five years, he traveled across the Midwest. He earned money by sending telegraph messages. And he thought about how to improve telegraphs.

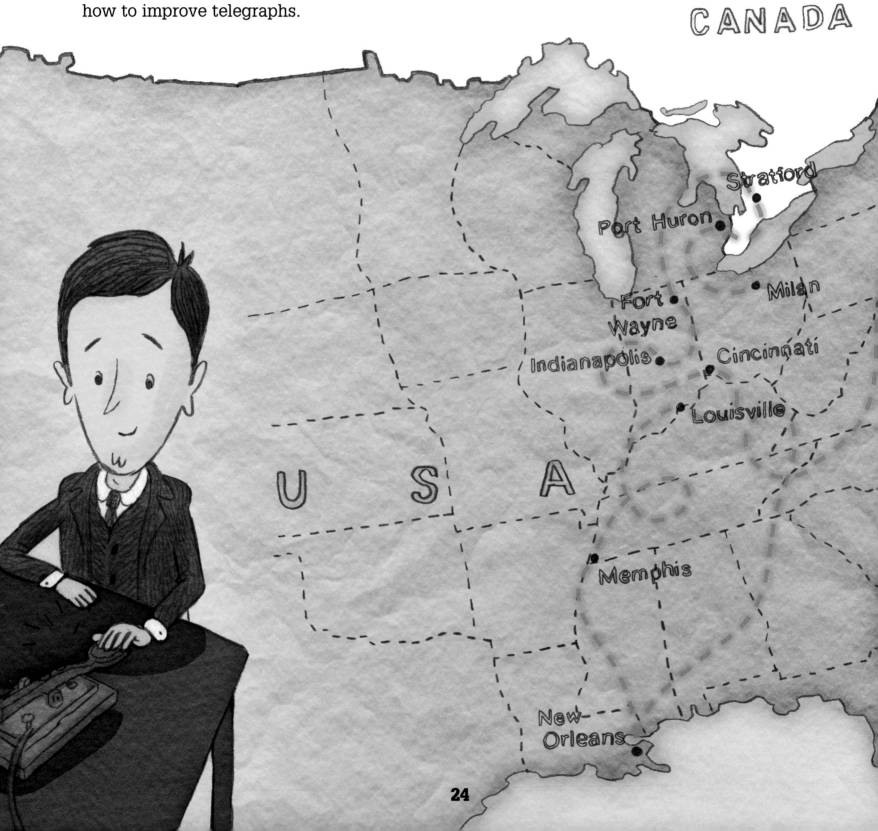

CANADA

Stratford

Port Huron

Milan

Fort Wayne

Cincinnati

Indianapolis

Louisville

U S A

Memphis

New Orleans

When Thomas wasn't working, he read and thought about science. He enjoyed carefully observing the people and machines around him.

Boston

New York

ATLANTIC OCEAN

To Thomas, the world was a very, very interesting place.

Even as Thomas Edison grew up, he never lost the wonder he felt as a child. He never stopped asking questions. More importantly, he never stopped working to answer them. Thomas felt that hard work, the ability to keep trying, and common sense were needed to achieve a goal.

When he was an old man, Thomas once told a group of school children,
"I am not a genius. Any success that I have had in life is due to hard work. Success is 98 percent hard work and sticking at the job until it is completed."

AFTERWORD

A list of everything Thomas Edison invented and accomplished could fill a very thick book. The following are just a few of his most famous accomplishments. Edison invented and improved a machine that helped people keep track of the stock market. At age 24, he sold it for $35,000. Later Edison invented a telegraph called the quadruplex that could send four signals, two in each direction. He sold this invention for even more money.

Thomas Edison was most famous for inventing the phonograph and the electric lightbulb. He set up a company to deliver electrical power for his lightbulbs. Over the years this company grew into one of the largest companies in the world.

A battery for an electric car and a motion picture camera were two of Thomas Edison's later inventions. He invented and created even into his 80s. He never stopped doing the things he did as a child—observing, wondering, questioning, and solving-problems. When he died in 1931, people dimmed the lights in their homes and buildings. They wanted to honor Thomas Edison as the man who helped bring much light to the world.

GLOSSARY

achieve—to accomplish; to bring to a successful end

chemistry—the scientific study of substances and their composition

curious—eager to explore and learn about new things

experiment—a scientific test to find out how something works

inquisitive—curious

invent—to think up and make something new

knack—a special skill or talent

observe—to watch someone or something closely in order to learn something

phonograph—a machine that plays sounds that have been recorded in the grooves of a record; a record has recorded sound or music

Seidlitz powder—bubbling salts made up of sodium bicarbonate, Rochelle salt, and tartaric acid; the powder was mixed with water as a type of medicine

stock market—a place where the buying and selling of stocks is held

telegraph—a machine that uses electrical signals to send messages over long distances

theory—an idea that explains something that is unknown

READ MORE

Barretta, Gene. *Timeless Thomas: How Edison Changed Our Lives*. New York: Henry Holt, 2012.

Kramer, Barbara. *Thomas Edison*. Washington, D.C.: National Geographic, 2014.

Spengler, Kremena. *An Illustrated Timeline of Inventions and Inventors*. Mankato, Minn.: Picture Window Books, 2012.

CRITICAL THINKING WITH THE COMMON CORE

1. What character qualities did Thomas show as a young man that helped him become successful? Give two or three examples and tell where you found them in the text. (Key Ideas and Details)

2. The author says that Thomas was always asking questions, and also trying to answer them. Give three examples of questions that he asked and tell how he tried to answer his own questions. (Integration of Knowledge and Ideas)

3. Name two events that changed Thomas' life. Describe how and why they changed his life, supporting your answers with passages from the text. (Key Ideas and Details)

INTERNET SITES

FactHound offers a safe, fun way to find Internet sites related to this book. All of the sites on FactHound have been researched by our staff.

Here's all you do:

Visit *www.facthound.com*

Type in this code: 9781479596836

Check out projects, games and lots more at
www.capstonekids.com

Other Titles in this Series

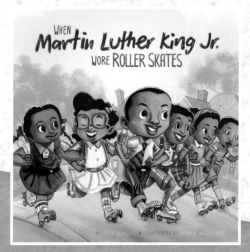

INDEX

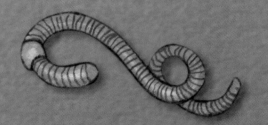

Special thanks to our adviser for his advice and expertise:
Paul Israel, Director and General Editor
Thomas A. Edison Papers, Rutgers University

Editor: Shelly Lyons
Designer: Ted Williams
Creative Director: Nathan Gassman
Production Specialist: Tori Abraham
The illustrations in this book were created with pencils, watercolors, and Photoshop.

Editor's Note: Direct Quotations are indicated by **bold** words.
Direct Quotations are found on the following pages:
page 5, line 1: Baldwin, Neil. Edison: Inventing the Century. New York: Hyperion, 2001.
Page 27: "4,000 School Children Attend Edison Party": Fort Myers Press. Fort Myers, Fla., Feb 11, 1928.

Picture Window Books are published by Capstone,
1710 Roe Crest Drive, North Mankato, Minnesota 56003
www.mycapstone.com

Library of Congress Cataloging-in-Publication Data
Names: Weakland, Mark. | Radcliffe, Thomas, illustrator.
Title: When Thomas Edison fed someone worms / by Mark Weakland ; illustrated by Thomas Radcliffe.
Description: North Mankato, Minnesota : Picture Window Books, 2017. | Series:
Leaders doing headstands | Audience: Grades 4 to 6. | Includes bibliographical references.
Identifiers: LCCN 2015050709
ISBN 9781479596836 (library binding)
ISBN 9781515801351 (paperback)
ISBN 9781515801436 (eBook PDF)
Subjects: LCSH: Edison, Thomas A. (Thomas Alva), 1847-1931—Childhood and youth—Juvenile literature. |
Inventors—United States—Biography—Juvenile literature. | Electrical engineers—United States—Biography—
Juvenile literature.
Classification: LCC TK140.E3 W39 2017 | DDC 621.3092—dc23
LC record available at http://lccn.loc.gov/2015050709

Printed in the United States   6012